Summary Of The Covenant of Water

Anthony F. Lujan

Content

Introduction

Three generations of a South Indian family are characterized by desires and transgressions, circumstances and aspirations, and divine and medical interventions.

"Where the sea meets the white sand, it thrusts fingers inland to entwine with the rivers meandering down the green-canopied slopes of the Ghats.

The setting's landscape is mirrored in Verghese's story, which is a confusing web of intertwining plots and enormous, intricate histories. Nevertheless, as one of the characters observes, "You can't set out to achieve your goals without a little madness." A 12-year-old girl gets married off to a widower with a little son in 1900, and this is when the lunacy starts. Before she turns thirteen, she will be referred to as Ammachi, the "little mother." Her life is the main stream that runs through the vast landscape of this tale, where drowning is merely the most typical of the terrible fates Verghese metes out to his beloved characters—burning, impaling, leprosy, opium addiction, hearing loss, smallpox, birth defects, political fanaticism, and so much more—even though many will also be given extraordinary gifts in the form of artistic ability, intellect, strength, and prophecy. The medical procedures and advancements play a prominent role in Verghese's (a physician) fiction debut, Cutting for Stone (2009), as they did in that book's best-selling and equally important predecessor. Scenes of hand surgery and brain surgery are described in the same eager detail as scenes of romantic encounters. Is all this essential at some points during this incredibly lengthy journey? one might quickly ponder. What a delight it is to state that one can feel the beautiful, wholly literary delight of all the puzzle pieces coming together in a way that

one genuinely does not anticipate. Ammachi realizes by the time she becomes a grandmother in the 1970s that "a good story goes beyond what a forgiving God cares to do.
God help us, he's done it again.

Chapter 1

The water that surrounds them, as well as other problems that trouble them, seem to have plagued this family for generations. This is a narrative of family.

Beginning in 1900, in Travancore, South India, with a girl who will be married the following morning, their story is set there. On this night, the final night she would ever spend in her sole home, her mother is lying next to her. The following morning, she wakes up early and, while her mother is still sleeping, sits down to write her thoughts, "her father's ghostly impression preserved in the cane weave," as she looks out the window and bids farewell to the lagoon, the coconut palms, and the creek. She has not yet met her future spouse, but she does know that he respects her because she is the daughter of a priest, even if "Her father's breath was now just air." With a small son and a widowed status, her future husband is forty years older than her. Twelve years old.

"Where the sea meets the white sand, it extends fingers inland to entwine with the rivers meandering down the green-canopied slopes of the Ghats."

Although this story covers the lives of many people, generations, and locations, the connections made and lost, as well as tragedies, it may appear at times that the individual stories aren't connected. However, the heart of this story is about connections, and eventually the individual stories, like the waters, all flow into one.

Abraham Verghese recently published an epic work of historical fiction that, according to a message to his readers, is based on the tales of his own mother. Between 1900 and 1977, it takes place in Kerala, India. We learn about the Parambil family and their shocking secret: every generation going back decades has lost a family member to drowning.

The narrative is so deep and vivid. Along with complex family dynamics, friendships, and romantic relationships, it also addresses social problems like the caste system and a country's right to self-determination.

"....[W]hen Just four days have passed since I finished the book, when I looked up. However, during that time I went through three generations and learned more about the world and myself than I do in a school year. The truth!

Chapter 2

The three generations of a family in Southern India are followed over the course of this grand novel. The family has many secrets, but the one that may be the most puzzling is why at least one family member every generation drowns. I feel as though I have spent all those years walking beside the characters because the story is written so exquisitely and because they are so rich and lively. Their lives cross and link like the water crosses and unites the land. Through that literary trapdoor you enter a world in which you will remain enthralled for the following 70 years. It starts in 1900 in India with the marriage of a 12-year-old girl to a widower who is several years her elder. The author skillfully weaves the tale of several seemingly unrelated characters with such wisdom and clarity as it moves from the quiet of Parambil to the back alleys of Glasgow, until it reaches the most intensely moving and heartbreaking conclusion, which, in my opinion, emphasizes the novel's most important lesson: none of us is alone. We are all one, as one of my favorite characters, Rune, who dedicates his life to helping people who don't belong, put it. The water, the land, the master, and the beggar. We don't actually have borders separating us. That epiphany led to the question of where we belong, where we are accepted for who we really are, and whether we will ever be able to live without being judged. This is measured by carefully evaluating the silent prejudices that lurk in even the most well-intentioned minds, as well as by highlighting the devastation caused by leprosy and the ongoing injustice of the caste system.

. It felt like a bereavement to finish this book. These characters had left, and I would never see them again. I had shared their joy, their sorrow, and my tears for the catastrophes they had to face for seventy years, and I genuinely wasn't ready to say goodbye. The final lesson I learned from this book is that people who came before us paved the way we now travel. This is excellently illustrated by the book's journey through the development of medicine (which includes the most wonderful explanation of the inflammatory cascade, which would have spared me months of uncertainty as a medical student). The hardships and sacrifices made by earlier generations—generations that can be found in both our own life and in the pages of a book—have made our journey so much easier. I might have to say goodbye to Digby, Shamuel, Big Ammachi, and Rune, but the joy they brought me and the lessons they taught me will always be with me.

This epic tale spanned several generations and was primarily set in India's Malabar area. I really enjoyed learning about the ceremonies and how, contrary to what I would have thought, these traditions had many advantages. A twelve-year-old girl is forced to wed a 40-year-old guy in the beginning. Sounds awful, but the situation turns out to be lovely and provides the plot's starting point. Since each character has been so thoroughly fleshed out, they are just like my friends and I, who detest moving on to the next scenario. until I ran into the following characters. I was able to visualize India because to this book. I can clearly see both the good and bad sides of this nation now. The varying time periods and characters were very enjoyable to me. Really pushes my thinking and keeps me alert. I enjoy how lengthy the book is.

Water's Covenant
Although the story starts in 1900, the history of the setting, which is present-day Kerala, dates back to 52 AD, when St. Thomas first set foot in this region of southern India. He evangelized them, and their descendants continue to practice Christianity now.

One family, the Parambils, could go back seven generations and found that at least one member of the family drowned in each generation. Although they all disliked water, these people all perished in bizarre water-related accidents. They sought to keep it a secret from anyone outside the family and referred to it as the Condition.

We highlight several Parambil generations. Mariamma finally makes the decision to go medical school and become a neurosurgeon. She was raised by her father and grandmother after her mother abandoned her soon after the birth of the child. Mariamma searches for the reason why so many of her family members have perished due to the Condition after her father passes away. She uncovers the answer to several secrets during her hunt, including one that is very personal to her.

In addition to being a neurosurgeon, the author has Keralan origin. He gives highly detailed depictions of this region of the world. He frequently went to see his grandparents throughout the summer. In order to unravel the riddle of the Condition, he also draws on his experience in medicine. The reader will typically recall this story long after it has ended. This novel, which was published 15 years after the author's best-selling Cutting for Stone, is worth the wait because the author is a superb storyteller.

Chapter 3

I couldn't help but worry if the author would be able to write another masterpiece after reading Cutting For Stone. I congratulate him for creating another masterpiece after just finishing its more than 700 pages. The Covenant of Water is a story about a family that goes through joy and pain, success and hardship, sickness, death, and occasionally a near-miraculous recovery over the course of about 70 years. It is set in the southern Indian state of Kerala and is partially based on tales told to him by his mother (and written out by her for her first granddaughter). It's a family with secrets, some held securely by a small number of people and some more publicly known. It's full of fascinating characters who are all flawed and imperfect but, in their own unique ways, are all trying to live the best lives they can. In addition, the book contains a lot of historical detail about how India changed over the 20th century as well as developments in the author's own medical specialty. All throughout, the writing is exquisite. Without any hesitation, I heartily suggest this book.

From start to finish, it's a fantastic narrative. One family's history from 1900 to 1977 in Kerala, South India, is the thread through which its varied themes, victories, and tragedies are woven. Verghese is an excellent writer, and his literary abilities come through in his painstaking, vivid descriptions of landscapes and civilizations, the construction of unforgettable, varied characters, some of which one cannot help but love, and in engaging, traditional storytelling. Verghese is a well-known internal medicine doctor and Stanford Professor, as most readers are probably aware, and this book, like Cutting for Stone, is infused with his passion to the wonders and mysteries of medicine.

This narrative has an impact on so many levels, from its underlying themes to the characters' unique personalities—both the disturbed and the likeable ones. Those who now feel like a part of my life, like Big Ammachi and Baby Mol, make me happy. The title refers to a disease known as simply "the Condition," which affects the main family, permeates the plot, and is responsible for a large portion of the acts of the characters. It causes fear of water and drownings, among other symptoms. Although its cause is unknown, it appears to be congenital. Even though this is obviously not a mystery novel, solving that riddle is part of the plot. I adore the book's portrayal of love, both its most heartwarming moments and occasionally tragic results, as well as the way its many (and varied!) individuals come together, split apart, and then re-unite. And I value how the author gently weaves this theme—which appears throughout the story—into the narrative, illustrating how much of each person's life is a product of the many generations who came before and how history shapes the present.

Between one group of characters and another, there is a good lot of switching. Readers will get the impression that eventually, even if this may initially be (only briefly) disorienting, all of these lives will somehow intertwine. Additionally, this book is lengthy (756 pages), and occasionally I wished it would move more quickly or wondered if it could have been cut down. However, for me, the last 20–25% just took off in such a rush that I couldn't put the book down. I was happy to have read the entire story because by the time it was over, I had a new understanding for it all. In terms of value for money across my whole reading career, few books compare to this one. Really, it is magnificent.

How does Covenant of Water work? Well, it contains elements of love, faith, family, and medicine. Note from the Author

Such memories are sewn with thin threads, and time eats holes in the fabric, which she must patch with myth and legend.

Abraham Verghese, the author of Cutting for Stone, finally published his long-awaited second book, and the wait was worthwhile! One landowning family in southern coastal India is followed through the 1900s in The Covenant of Water. A strange illness that this family also has makes their relationship with water complicated.

Whether writing about scenery, medical procedures, or family dynamics, Verghese's writing was incredibly rich in detail. The thorough descriptions of challenging operations are undoubtedly provided by a skilled author. I lost myself in it entirely.

Chapter 4

A grand work of literature that reflects the author's love of India and her people.

The family that a 12-year-old girl who becomes known as Big Ammachi marries into around the turn of the century harbors a lot of secrets. After her father passed away, her uncle now decides what will happen to the girl and her mother, and a marriage broker sets them up with a widower who is considerably older than she is. Big Ammachi adores her husband's tiny kid JoJo, and the marriage turns out to be joyful. Despite how much she misses her mother, she eventually learns to enjoy Parambil in Kerala on the Malabar coast of South India. In every generation, at least one member of her husband's family suffers a severe aversion to water and perishes by drowning; the illness that causes this perplexing affliction becomes known as "The Condition." The fact that their land is encircled by water makes this horrible fate all but inevitable, and Big Ammachi learns this secret only after catastrophe strikes. Years pass, and India experiences transformation as it rebels against British control, sends boys to fight in World War II, and earns freedom. The rigid caste system in India begins to relax at least a little, but not everyone benefits equally, and there are upheavals against the dominant castes. Big Ammachi and her family are in love, quarrel, get married, have kids, and go through catastrophes, but they still maintain their faith, their tight-knit family ties, and their love for Parambil.

A novel's plot cannot be condensed into a single paragraph when it has more than 700 pages. A intergenerational family saga with a strong feeling of place, The Covenant of Water is an epic story that brought to mind the works of James Michener or Colleen McCullough. I knew very little about this region of India or the Christian community that lives there when I started the book. I discovered a lot about both through Dr. Verghese's story, as well as a friendly elephant, a leper colony, and a doctor from poor circumstances who journeys from Glasgow to India in search of a surgical career. Although by no means an easy read, I thought the book was eminently enjoyable. It was enjoyable to lose myself in the lavish storyline while getting to know and care for each eccentric character. Big Ammachi experiences a lot of upheaval, social unrest, and personal tragedy over the course of her life, yet the book is not depressing since the characters still have hope. They remain strong in the face of difficulty and anticipate happier times.

I highly recommend that anyone who enjoyed reading "Cutting for Stone" pick up a copy of Abraham Verghese's most recent book. If you enjoy reading authors like Michener, Clavell, or McCullough, I strongly suggest you give this a shot. The reader will be rewarded with an enthralling plot and characters that will linger with them long after the last page has been read if they are willing to make the time commitment.

Chapter 5

The Covenant of Water, which spans the years 1900–1977, depicts three generations of a family living in a small Christian village in Kerala who are affected by an odd condition. The tale starts in 1900, when a 12-year-old girl marries a guy who is considerably older than she is, and she moves home with him and his son on the family estate. She acquires the name large Ammachi as an adult, which is Malayalam for "big mother" and is the language used in Kerala. Big Ammachi quickly discovers that her husband and her husband's extended family are afflicted by a mysterious illness that causes an aversion to water, which is remarkable given that they reside close to Kerala's rivers and backwaters. Big Ammachi is motivated to solve this mystery in order to save her children and eventually her grandkids after discovering that at least one person each generation has perished by drowning on an old genealogy chart. The common thread in her life—which includes both enormous joy and devastating tragedy—is her determination to discover a treatment for her illness. In the book's latter chapters, a parallel story of a Glaswegian physician named Digby Kilgour traveling to India to practice surgery intersects and converges a few times.

Although Big Ammachi's life is the focus of this story, it is woven with a lot more than just family, love, and loss. The story spans nearly eight decades and touches on issues like poverty, the caste system, religion, and women's rights. It also covers the history of South India and the creation of the state of Kerala, including politics and the rise of communism in Kerala after independence. Leprosy, childbirth, and neurosurgery are a few other fascinating medical topics that are important to the plot and relate to understanding the Condition at the center of the book. The lyrical wording is lovely throughout, but I really like the descriptive descriptions of Kerala's terrain, which helped me visualize the story's setting.

Big Ammachi is twelve years old when she marries the Parambil household. Her husband is a forty-year-old widower with a young child. There's a mystery in his family. They have a history of drownings where at least one person has perished suddenly per generation. The avoidance of water was a lifelong habit among those people, and it appears that this behavior is inherited. Since water is a part of everyone's life in Kerala, a state with many water features, it is difficult to believe such a thing until Big Ammachi loses a loved one herself one day. She then asks God to either send someone who can cure her "Condition" (as the family refers to it) or to heal her herself. Will God answer her prayers, or will tragedies continue to occur? This is a three generation narrative, beginning in 1900 and ending in 1977.

Given the length of this book, I was a little intimidated as I was ready to begin it. The author's writing abilities, though, were sufficient to dispel this bias. Even though I've been to Kerala before, the way he described the scenery has made me long to go there again.

The book gives readers a glimpse into daily life in a Malayalam household.

The author's descriptions of India during British administration are likewise accurate. The novel has a lot of medical terminology and anatomical descriptions, but they work well with the plot and do not detract from the story.

The story's key themes include love and the connection between family members.

Given the lengthy timeline of the plot, there are a sizable number of characters.

However, as the narrative develops, the reader will get to know them, making it easier for them to be connected to the story. I was amazed by how the author explained medical words such that people who are not medical professionals would have no trouble understanding.

Even though it's a family saga, there's a lot of suspense in this book that will have you turning the pages until the very end. For all fans of fiction, it is a must-read.

Chapter 6

The Covenant of Water was a massive examination at a family line in a Christian family who lived in a settlement near the southern tip of India that spanned about 8 decades and 736 pages. The author, a doctor who has also written other books including Cutting for Stone, writes both analytically and lyrically. His passion of medicine is evident in the subjects discussed in this narrative, and the wording is lovely despite occasionally being a little too technical.

One of my all-time favorite books is Cutting for Stone, so when I saw that a new family tale was being published, I was thrilled. It was simple for time to pass without my realizing because of the story's numerous depths and captivating nature. Some of the characters made me fall in love, and I found the medical aspect of the story to be quite fascinating.

The concept of a gene-based condition that manifests as a fear of water and a propensity to drowning was innovative. In Kerala, the setting of the novel, drownings account for more than 14% of all pediatric fatalities. Water can be found in rivers, rushing through canals, and along the shoreline along the Malabar Coast.

The many topics Verghese addresses include colonialism and independence, disability, family and intergenerational relationships, caste systems, medicine, addiction, poverty, catastrophe, and politics.

Overall, I thought this was a book I could learn from, one that led me down the rabbit hole of Google, one that required notes (for me), had nice transitions, and allowed me to appreciate going back and reading the minor details from the plot that later were significant. It was also quite slow-moving and lengthy, but if you have the patience, I believe it will be worth it in the end.

I had no idea where the narrative would lead me when it opened in Southern India in 1900. In the beginning, a young bride is caring for her older husband and his toddler when she discovers that she is joining a family that has a peculiar illness that causes generations of drownings, even in the shallowest of water. As she grows older, she transforms into large Ammachi (large mother) and learns how to parent while realizing that anything could happen to any of her family members. In addition, as the matriarch of her town, she is concerned for many people in addition to her own children. Through the generations of Big Ammachi's family, her small village, and Verghese's exquisite writing, the reader is guided through India's history.

A leper colony, an Irish doctor's life in India, and some of the most endearing people I've read in a while are also explored. Of course, we also learn about the history of medicine, just like in Cutting for Stone.

This is an epic family novel entwining many characters in its web. The only thing I could say is that it might have used a little editing, but because of how beautifully he uses language, I didn't mind the extra word count.

This did not let me down in any way on the literary side of things because I enjoy stories that bring all the characters together and come full circle at the end.

Chapter 7

Beginning at the turn of the twentieth century and up until the 1970s, the Convenant of Water is the epic saga of the Parambils of India, who can date their family heritage back seven generations. They are St Thomas Christians living as a minority community in what is largely a Hindu culture.

When Mariamma is twelve years old she is married off to a much older widower with a young son. As the story grows, so does the number of family members. Each has his or her own particular story with two constant threads interweaving the generations. The first is that the family seems to have a curse in that offspring are likely to die by drowning. Why and how this is so is a mystery. The second thread is the pull toward the practice of medicine for many family members.

Verghese is a master of brilliant flowing, almost poetic prose, written with passion.

His first book, Cutting For Stone was a masterpiece. I so looked forward to this one but it fell short, as it was exceedingly looooong and lost my interest at times, only to engage me again at other times. I felt like there might be more than one book here that would have held up better in separate volumes.

On the plus side, the author was able to immerse me in the rigorous training in which doctors must partake. I felt I was there. He compassionately described the life and trials of lepers. Love stories abound and add a warm and beautiful personal flavor. The plight of India as an possession of outsiders, and the internal fight for independence and then division is clearly drawn. In fact so many important issues reside in this huge saga that it would be impossible to credit all of them.

It truly hurts me to rate this book three stars. It was the unevenness of the read that drives my rating. For me it was a great writer, writing more than the story warranted. Yet, I'm glad I read it.

I remember slowly being drawn into the narrative of Cutting for Stone, Verghese's previous novel that came out more than a decade ago. And when you start The Covenant of Water, the mastery of the novel helps you understand why we had to wait so long for another masterpiece. (That and the fact that Verghese is an MD and professor.

The Covenant of Water follows a multigenerational family in India from 1900 to 1977. It follows Big Ammachi ("Big Mother") from a young bride through multiple generations of her family. It's partly about "the condition" in which members of her family throughout the generations dies by drowning. But it's also about family and strength and love, both marital and between parent and child. As an MD Verghese infuses deep medical knowledge throughout, but it's fascinating.

Conclusion

This wonderful book discussed family, secrets, almost religions, life, love, pain, and death. Politics and the division of individuals by artificial barriers were the main topics. It dealt with chasing after dreams, both succeeding and failing.

The characters in this fantastic tale were vivid and full of life. Characters with a strong sense of compassion, devotion, and family. Yes, while reading this book, I shed a few tears.

It was a novel about water. Choose this book to read if you read just one book this year.

Made in United States
Troutdale, OR
04/21/2024